AF472580

21 Day Positivity Challenge

To Eliminate Stinking Thinking

Rachon Thomas

▼A Royal Touch Book▼

ISBN 978-1-105-96844-0

Printed in the United States of America

For my Mom and Dad, my Father,
my Grandmother,
my Son Joshua, my Daughter Azjahnae
and my Siblings...
Winston Jr.
Bryan David
Kimberly Nicole
Tiffany Lynne

And to My Apostle Dr. JoAnn Long
For speaking this into my life 3 years ago.

21 Day Positivity Challenge

To Eliminate Stinking Thinking

Author's Note

Thank you to all of my loved ones, family and friends who have supported me in my endeavors throughout the years. My hope is that you will be able to walk away from this challenge refreshed and renewed in your thinking. This journey stemmed from a personal challenge that was God-inspired during a 40 day consecration. The fast was a journey through Psalms 37 with my spiritual mentor and Godmother Evangelist Dorothy McCullough. While in prayer the Lord spoke a word for us to not only do the fast but for me to challenge myself in the way I normally think and process things. I accepted the instruction and took the challenge day by day. I had no idea a real change would take place and propel me to a totally different way of thinking. In the end, I was able to look back and appreciate the perseverance as there were many instances throughout this 21 Day Challenge that I truly wanted to give up. My mentor encouraged me, and two challenges in one later this particular challenge was birthed out it all.

I want to say thank you now for stepping out on your faith and taking this 21 Day challenge with me. It's a personal journey within itself that can be repeated numerous times. I hope you enjoy the ride.

-Rachon, May 2011

ঌ A Prayer Before We Begin ঌ

Lord, as I have been obedient to your will in sharing what you have given for my own personal growth, I pray for a life shaking change among your people. I pray that your will be done in each person who desires a lifestyle change in their thinking. I pray for your anointing to rest on every page of this journey. I pray that each day as the challenges are taken, the affirmations are read and the thoughts are absorbed that your spirit takes complete control. I decree and declare that your power shall cause every negative thought and situation to be changed and eliminated in Jesus name.

Amen!

Introduction

Statistics show that 80 - 90% of our thoughts are negative.

As human beings we have the option of thinking positively, negatively or indifferent. Within our 3000 thoughts daily we have the ability to control not only what flows through our spirit man but also what flows through the atmosphere around us. Have you ever walked into a room with a huge smile and those in the room smile back at you?

On the flip side if you have ever walked into a room with a frown or uncertain look on your face almost instantly you get quick glances, return frowns or even whispers from those who pick up on the perceived energy you're giving off.

In most cases, what you're surrounded by is what you tend to exhibit. Someone surrounded by negativity can easily generate that negative energy and a person surrounded by peaceful energy certainly has the ability to generate the same.

Growing up I had a picky personality and always wanted things done just right. If they weren't done to my standards then I had no problem offering my opinion of how things could have been done better. With that said, the energies I put forth in correcting were at times not positive.

There were times when my negativity was taken humorously by friends as this was my way to camouflage my thoughts. And while some of my friends got a good kick out of my off the wall comments and didn't take them to heart, they were most times my truest feelings.

In my thirties is when I really began to notice my thought pattern. Instead of exerting the extra energy to find what was good in a situation, I would sometimes expound on the first negative thought that entered my mind.

The desire to change for me came after I began to get serious about continuing my education and attended some seminars on empowerment. The reflection of the people who spoke was so powerful and captivating that I was able to pick up on their energy and mirror this energy while in their presence. However, the minute I was out of that particular environment my thoughts would eventually migrate back to "the norm".

Spiritually, I was always able to flourish
in my encouragement of others,
but could not seem to apply those same thoughts
to the way I perceived situations in my own life.

It wasn't until I enrolled in a parenting class while pursuing my bachelors that I learned of behavior modifications. In simplest form this was achieved by replacing an unwanted behavior with a welcomed or more positive behavior.

Have you ever heard the saying that doing something for 21 days can negatively or positively create a habit? Well the purpose of this journal is to create a 21 day road map to the elimination of stinking thinking.

The exercises can be repeated over and over again until the mindset changes and hopefully becomes second hand nature. With this in mind, let's focus on the perception of changing from the inside out as opposed to changing from the outside in.

It is my hope that after these 21 days you will be able to think more positively by focusing your thoughts on more positive things.

Let's start with a scripture...

And be not conformed to this world: but be ye transformed by the renewing of your mind, that ye may prove what is that good, and acceptable, and perfect, will of God.
Romans 2:2 (KJV)

21 Day Positivity Challenge

To Eliminate Stinking Thinking

WELCOME

TO THE 21 DAY POSITIVITY CHALLENGE TO ELIMINATE STINKING THINKING

☙CHALLENGER INSTRUCTIONS☙

A challenge is a call to engage in a contest, fight or competition.

What is the contest? To complete this entire challenge. What are we fighting? Resistance to changing our thinking. Who are we competing against? Our inner selves.

The challenge will consist of a daily thought, an affirmation and of course a daily challenge. Should you miss a day jump back in. Some days will be lighter than others and some days may truly be a test...

→There will be a daily Challenger Check in poll asking: ←

Did you recite today's Commitment Statement?
Did you recite the Daily Affirmation?
Did you take the Positivity Challenge?

Note: You will need sticky notes for Day 5. There is also a journal area in which you can keep track of your daily thoughts for personal reflection. Ask someone to partner with you on this journey to assist you in staying motivated. Let's train our brain...and eliminate stinking thinking! Your thoughts create your destiny! Let's Go!

ೋContentsೋ

WEEK ONE

Day 1

༄

IT'S A GREAT DAY

Statistics say: 80-90% of our thoughts are negative. Today is the first day of our 21 days of positive thinking which will ultimately aid in the achievement of eliminating stinking thinking!

Have you ever heard of a behavior modification plan? Well it simply calls for the monitoring of an unwanted behavior and the replacing of that same behavior repeatedly with something positive. Eventually the unwanted behavior is replaced.

Today you may have to constantly remind yourself that you have embarked on a proactive journey of self improvement, so take a deep breath.

Let's begin with a COMMITMENT STATEMNT and affirmation aloud:

Today I embark upon my 21 day journey
of eliminating stinking thinking!
20 days from now my thoughts will be less toxic
and more abundantly positive!
I am committed to changing my way of thinking!

ꕥ IT'S A GREAT DAY ꕥ
AFFIRMATION

Today is a great day, my life is great, my love is Great and it's flowing, can you feel my flow?!!!

Write this affirmation on something you will see throughout your day and continuously repeat it. Text this message to some of your friends, and post this to your status on your social networking site. When someone asks how your day is going try responding with all or parts of the affirmation statement above.

Now this is contagious so let's make it spread... And remember not to let anyone or anything pull you off your square!

ꕥ IT'S A GREAT DAY ꕥ
CHALLENGE

Your only challenge today is to get the positive energy flowing around you. Get some sun, smile, laugh, give a compliment, open up communication with someone, be pleasant and at the end of the day reflect on how well your day went.
Now let's go!!!

ଔ IT'S A GREAT DAY REFLECTION ଔ

Reflect on your day...
What type of energy did you experience?

____

____

____

____

____

____

____

____

____

____

- ✓ **Did you recite today's Commitment Statement?**
- ✓ **Did you recite today's Affirmation?**
- ✓ **Did you take the Day 1 Challenge?**
- ✓ **Did you share the challenge with someone else?**

Day 2

ஒஒ

COMMAND YOUR DAY
SPEAK TO IT!

To command means to give an order or demand with authority.

Each and every day you can COMMAND YOUR DAY & charge the atmosphere by SPEAKing into it. Should it start to sidetrack just remind it and yourself of your early morning command...

Yesterday is now gone and today is a new day! So speak those things that be not as though they were! Utilize your power!

Commitment Statement:

Today I embark upon my 2nd day's journey of eliminating stinking thinking...19 days from now my thoughts will be less toxic and more abundantly positive! I am committed to changing MY WAY of thinking!

☙ COMMAND YOUR DAY ☙
AFFIRMATION

I HAVE THE POWER WITHIN TO CHANGE THE ATMOSPHERE AROUND ME!

Now make a COMMAND on YOUR DAY...
TAKE OWNERSHIP OF IT!

(No matter what...I will not allow anyone or anything, to steal my peace today). And remember not to let anyone or anything pull you off your square! Keep in mind your command will most likely be challenged...

WHEN the test comes, release all *stinking thinking* from your mind and
LET IT GO!

How do you release? By telling yourself this is just a test and by recognizing there is more than one way to react.

Tell yourself "I will not be moved by what I see, hear or feel but only by what I know!"

Remember you must be open to changing "your norm" of thinking.

Release any anger, frustration or anxiety that may rise up and repeat aloud today's affirmation AND your command.

☙ COMMAND YOUR DAY ☙ CHALLENGE

Think of a situation that you know you need to handle in a different manner. Give yourself 3 positive ways to approach or 3 positive ways in which to respond. Let's go!!!

☙ COMMAND YOUR DAY ☙

Reflect on your day...

✓ Did you recite today's Commitment Statement?
✓ Did you recite today's Affirmation?
✓ Did you take the Day 2 Challenge?
✓ Did you share the challenge with someone else?

Day 3

ꕥꕥ

Commitment Statement:

Today I embark upon my 3rd day's journey of eliminating stinking thinking…18 days from now my thoughts will be less toxic and more abundantly positive! I am fully committed to changing my way of thinking!

CHEERFUL GIVER DAY

It's a wonderful day and it's truly a blessing to give!!! As we become givers (for some) and cheerful givers (for others) it is reciprocated or returned!

There's nothing worse than giving out of a poor spirit or attitude. What can you give today? A kind word, a thought, a gesture, a few minutes of your time, knowledge, attention to someone who needs it.

Think of it as the planting of a seed in potted dirt which will develop and grow in time, bringing with it a harvest...and not necessarily in the same way that it was given; but in a manner that will meet a need perhaps for you, your spouse, your family or your children. Keep a positive mind and give SOMETHING today.

☙CHEERFUL GIVER ☙ AFFIRMATION

I am a cheerful giver. I give daily. I give of my substance, my talent, my time and my sprit. Giving is fulfilling!

Giving is a beautiful thing. And to be able to give is even more wonderful! Every single time I give I set myself up to receive a blessing.

☙ CHEERFUL GIVER ☙ CHALLENGE

Give something cheerfully today not out of necessity or begrudgingly, this should be done with thought and design (not half heartedly).

Try giving with a smile instead of a smirk, frown or pursed lips. Give with a kind gesture as opposed to sarcasm, cynicism or the "waiting to exhale" breath that comes just before...

Every man according as he purpose in his heart, so let him give; not grudgingly, or of necessity: for God loveth a cheerful giver. 2 Corinthians 9:7

☙ CHEERFUL GIVER ☙

Reflect on your day...

✓ Did you recite today's Commitment Statement?
✓ Did you recite today's Affirmation?
✓ Did you take the Day 3 Challenge?
✓ Did you share the challenge with someone else?

Day 4

ஃ

Commitment Statement:

Today I embark upon my 4th day's journey of eliminating stinking thinking...17 days from now my thoughts will be less toxic and more abundantly positive! I am fully committed to changing my way of thinking!

TAKE OFF DAY

Push past the resistance to change.
It's Day 4 of positive thinking to eliminate stinking thinking and by now you are sure to have felt the sting of resistance in changing the way you normally think about things. However, if I can do it, believe me you can too.

It's a new day and you are that much closer to a new you. You're an airplane on the runway and you're taking off (expect a little turbulence).

Let's really concentrate on the elimination of our own stinkn' thinkn' as we cannot regulate what others think or do.

ꙮ TAKE OFF AFFIRMATION ꙮ

I am on the runway and taking off...
I am pushing past the resistance to change
and eliminating stinking thinking.

Things that take off: Airplanes, eagles, rockets and so much more. Be the airplane, eagle and rocket that you are and soar past that ground thinking.

Let me repeat...this is not and will not be an easy task but to whom much is given much is required. Soon you will be able to have a POSITIVE effect on the world around you! Over time this thinking will become second hand nature and not something you have to really think about to do.

ꙮ TAKE OFF CHALLENGE ꙮ

SEE IT...WRITE IT...SAY IT

SEE IT... Close your eyes and envision yourself at a door called resistance, push past it and step through the door. WRITE IT... Write this statement... "I am pushing past the resistance to change!" SAY IT... Today at every onset of negative thinking, cancel it by saying to yourself or aloud, "I am pushing past the resistance to change and eliminating stinking thinking".

☙ TAKE OFF ☙

Reflect on your day…

____

____

____

____

____

____

____

____

____

____

____

- ✓ **Did you recite today's Commitment Statement?**
- ✓ **Did you recite today's Affirmation?**
- ✓ **Did you take the Day 4 Challenge?**
- ✓ **Did you share the challenge with someone else?**

Day 5

ꕥ

Commitment Statement:

Today I embark upon my 5th day's journey of eliminating stinking thinking…16 days from now my thoughts will be less toxic and more abundantly positive! I am fully committed to changing my way of thinking!

THE LITTLE ENGINE THAT COULD DAY

I think I can, I think I can, I think I can, I think I can…
I KNOW I CAN, I KNOW I CAN, I KNOW I CAN!
I KNOW I CAN!
(As a man thinketh so is he)

The *Little Engine that Could*, questioned his ability to make it up the hill, he eventually made it because of determination, stamina and constant reminders. And like the Little Engine you are successfully heading up hill. Good News! You are a quarter of the way there!!!! Let's celebrate with today's challenge.

☙ THE LITTLE ENGINE THAT COULD ☙ CHALLENGE

You will need your sticky notes for this one...

Make a list of affirmations you need to affirm daily. Each one should have its own sticky note. Once completed, place them EVERYWHERE!

On your bathroom mirror, the refrigerator, front door, dashboard of your car, on your wallet, on your day planner, your ipad and in every room of your house.

Each time that you see or pass by a sticky note stop and read that affirmation aloud.

Your AFFIRMATIONS must be personal.

Here are a few examples:

Today is a new day full of possibility;
New doors are open to me...

I forgive myself and others
And allow the past to rest in the past...

I will not allow my emotions to control me...
Feelings are fickle...

I live the best, drive the best and have the best
Because I am the best...

Nothing can work against me
Because everything is working for me...

I am a millionaire in the making
And today brings me one step closer...

No matter how I wake up
My day is full of promise and opportunity...

I am respectful of others
And will in turn receive the same...

☙THE LITTLE ENGINE THAT COULD ☙

Reflect on your day...

____

____

____

____

____

____

____

____

____

____

✓ **Did you recite today's Commitment Statement?**
✓ **Did you recite today's Affirmation?**
✓ **Did you take the Day 5 Challenge?**
✓ **Did you share the challenge with someone else?**

Day 6

ꕥꕥ

Commitment Statement:

Today I embark upon my 6th day's journey of eliminating stinking thinking…15 days from now my thoughts will be less toxic and more abundantly positive! I am fully committed to changing my way of thinking!

MIRROR ME DAY

This morning I woke up to my sticky notes of affirmations EVERYWHERE. As I approached each sticky note I stopped and read each one that I passed aloud. It was such an awesome uplift. Now when I hear affirmations from others it makes me SMILE!

Come on let's REFLECT:

Day 1: We made it a great day. Did you feel the initiation of the flow?

Day 2: We commanded our day and changed the atmosphere around us.

Day 3: We learned to be not only givers but cheerful givers.

Day 4: Was our take off day, we pushed past the resistance to change... and soared.

Day 5: We changed our "thinking we could" to "knowing we could" and made reminders.

☙ MIRROR ME ☙ CHALLENGE

Stand in the mirror and practice speaking to yourself. Go so far as to point to yourself as you're speaking. What are you speaking? Your affirmations and the opposite of any known flaws you might have.

Example:
I am more than a conqueror!

I am flowing in abundance
and no one can stop my flow!

Now I want you (after your first couple affirmations) to repeat those same affirmations looking directly into your own eyes and simply smile while doing it this time. Afterwards think about how that made you feel.

What you see in that mirror is exactly what you are reflecting. Now that you know what to do and how to do it, incorporate this into your morning ritual or your daily routine.

☙ MIRROR ME ☙ AFFIRMATION

TODAY IS GOING TO BE AN AWESOME DAY MY BLESSINGS ARE ALL AROUND ME. I'M REFLECTING WHAT I WANT OTHERS TO SEE! IN ACTUALITY I'M ASKING THEM TO MIRROR ME BECAUSE WHAT I GIVE OUT IS COMING BACK TO ME!

☙ MIRROR ME ☙

Reflect on your day...

✓ Did you recite today's Commitment Statement?
✓ Did you recite today's Affirmation?
✓ Did you take the Day 6 Challenge?
✓ Did you share the challenge with someone else?

Day 7

ஓஒ

Commitment Statement:

Today I embark upon my 7th day's journey of eliminating stinking thinking…14 days from now my thoughts will be less toxic and more abundantly positive! I am fully committed to changing my way of thinking!

A DAY OF SMILES

It's a beautiful day in the neighborhood and has the potential for a positivity explosion!

Brighten the room today with your smile it has the possibility of opening doors for your life and aids in eliminating stinking thinking. Such a beautiful thing!!!

A smile is a facial expression that is caused by flexing the muscles at the corners of one's mouth. Smiling elicits happy feelings and is understood by every culture; likewise…

a smile is a natural reaction to a positive experience.

☙ A DAY OF SMILES ☙ CHALLENGE

Today you will incorporate a smile into every portion of your day from the time you awake until the time you lay down tonight for sleep. This is the law of attraction. Have you ever noticed that when you smile at the world it smiles back at you? Likewise a frown at the world will cause just the opposite. Every place that you go today (permitting) let your smile proceed you.

Ask others to join in with your "Day of Smiles" today and watch the world become a brighter and more positive place around you.

How does this eliminate stinking thinking you ask? Well simply because it's difficult in nature to have stinking thinking while "positively" smiling.
Let's smile the day away!

☙ A DAY OF SMILES ☙ AFFIRMATION

Every time you smile at someone, it is an action of love, a gift to that person, a beautiful thing.
~ Mother Teresa

ઉ A DAY OF SMILES ઉ

Reflect on your day...

____

____

____

____

____

____

____

____

____

✓ **Did you recite today's Commitment Statement?**
✓ **Did you recite today's Affirmation?**
✓ **Did you take the Day 7 Challenge?**
✓ **Did you share the challenge with someone else?**

WEEK TWO

Day 8

ᔕᔕ

Commitment Statement:

Today I embark upon my 8th day's journey of eliminating stinking thinking…13 days from now my thoughts will be less toxic and more abundantly positive! I am fully committed to changing my way of thinking!

ONE MONKEY DOESN'T STOP THE SHOW

Challenger did you know that "***one monkey***" doesn't stop the show?

There's greatness deep down inside of each and every one of us. The degree of greatness may vary, but nonetheless it's still greatness and it just needs to be unlocked.

Some of us are equipped with the tools to unlock ourselves and have done so; others need the assistance of those we may come into contact with.

What does it take to unlock something? A key right? Well, simply put the right person will have the right key. Do not fret or be dismayed when something does not happen the way you "thought" it would, remember the old cliché "there's always more than one way to skin a cat".

That's why "one monkey" doesn't stop the show! So keep your head up and understand that you're just steps away from discovering the ONE with the RIGHT KEY. Remember some of us are able to unlock ourselves and others need the assistance of someone else to aid in unlocking them. Know that the lock contains YOUR GREATNESS!

Do we really know what greatness is? Greatness is dependent upon the percepted and subjective opinions of those who apply them.

One way to think of greatness is this: "... If any man desire to be first the same shall be last of all and servant of all."
Mark 9:35 KJV

T. Alan Armstrong says “If there is no passion in your life, then have you really lived?” Find your passion, whatever it may be, become it, and let it become you and you will find great things happen FOR you, TO you and through you.

Charles de Montesquieu says “To become truly great, one has to stand with people, not above them.“

With that said our
☙ ONE MONKEY ☙
DOESN’T STOP THE SHOW
AFFIRMATION for today is:

One monkey doesn’t stop the show
there’s greatness inside of me
and it’s unlocking my path to destiny
and taking me before great people.

☙ ONE MONKEY ☙
DOESN'T STOP THE SHOW

Reflect on your day...

____

____

____

____

____

____

____

____

____

____

- ✓ Did you recite today's Commitment Statement?
- ✓ Did you recite today's Affirmation?
- ✓ Did you take the Day 8 Challenge?
- ✓ Did you share the challenge with someone else?

Day9

Commitment Statement:

Today I embark upon my 9th day's journey of eliminating stinking thinking...12 days from now my thoughts will be less toxic and more abundantly positive! I am fully committed to changing my way of thinking!

I Won't Complain Day

The positivity flows until something happens and then *bam* a small complaint. Be aware of this and work to remove any and all complaining, while notably adding more sticky notes of affirmation today! You're well on your way to eliminating stinking thinking.

Soar through your day and be blessed!
Do all things without complaining and disputing. Phil 2:14 KJV

৯ I WON'T COMPLAIN ৯
AFFIRMATION

Today's affirmation will come from a popular Christian Gospel song entitled "I Won't Complain".

*I've had some good day's**
*and I've had some hills to climb**
*I've had some weary day's**
*and some lonely nights**
*but when I look around**
*and I think things over**
*all of my good days**
*they outweigh by bad days**
so I won't complain!!!

↜ I WON'T COMPLAIN ↜ CHALLENGE

Chant, meditate or recite: I won't complain, I won't complain, I won't complain, I won't complain (repeatedly)!

Try this on your drive in,
your morning walk,
your morning run,

your ride up in the elevator,
on the way to court,
sitting in the waiting room,

when that gossiping co-worker comes to your office/cubicle,
when you have to do someone else's job, while waiting on that next job,

picking up after a spouse or child,
when you're bored with nothing to do,

at school, while cleaning house,
fixing dinner and so on and so on...

☙ I WON'T COMPLAIN ☙

Reflect on your day...

- ✓ Did you recite today's Commitment Statement?
- ✓ Did you recite today's Affirmation?
- ✓ Did you take the Day 9 Challenge?
- ✓ Did you share the challenge with someone else?

Day10

ক্ক

Commitment Statement:

Today I embark upon my 10th day's journey of eliminating stinking thinking...11 days from now my thoughts will be less toxic and more abundantly positive! I am fully committed to changing my way of thinking!

Freedom to Forgive Day

Forgiveness is defined in the dictionary as the process of concluding resentment, indignation or anger as a result of a perceived offense, difference, mistake, or ceasing to demand punishment or restitution.

Anger is a natural emotion that can escalate into retaliation or root in bitterness. The key to forgiveness is a constant renewing of your mind to let go of unforgiveness and release that person, thing or incident causing you to continuously replay the misfortune over again in your mind.

Practice talking to yourself when you feel anger rising, JUST SAY NO! I have forgiven this person and will no longer allow anger or my emotions to overtake me as it relates to that incident.

Sometimes we have a desire to let go of something concerning a person or incident but just don't know how...

The solution? You guessed it "the changing of our mind" it's so much easier said than done but you'll never know if you never put forth the effort and try...

KNOW THAT YOU WIIL HAVE REMARKABLE RESULTS!

FREEDOM TO FORGIVE CHALLENGE

Sit quietly (no distractions) for at least 5 minutes and write on a napkin that can be disposed, the names of all those who have wronged you in some way.

Accept that now is the time for you to let go of ALL hurt and resentment, so that you may be released from unforgiveness.

Go through each name and remember for one last time what each person did or what they were the cause of in creating the unforgiveness in your life.

Now read each person's name from your list, state what it is that you are letting go of aloud and continue with each name until you reach the end of your list.

When you are ready, get up from where you are sitting and take the list with you to the washroom.

Say your last goodbyes
and flush this napkin away.

Now breathe

and recite today's affirmation.

☙ FREEDOM TO FORGIVE ☙ AFFIRMATION

Today I freely forgive myself
and others and let go of unwanted anger.
I am free to forgive, free to love,
free to grow, free to be me and free to live.

☙ FREEDOM TO FORGIVE PRAYER ☙

LORD, AS I LOOK AT EACH AND EVERY ONE OF THESE NAMES THAT I HAVE WRITTEN, I REMEMBER ONE LAST TIME THE THINGS THAT THEY HAVE DONE OR CAUSED TO HAPPEN IN MY LIFE.

I REMEMBER ONE LAST TIME TODAY TO CONSCIOUSLY REMEMBER NO MORE. LORD AS I READ EACH NAME IN SILENCE I AM ALLEVIATING AND ALLOWING THE BURDEN THAT THEY HAVE PLACED TO BE REMOVED.

FROM THIS DAY FORWARD I RELEASE AND LET GO OF ANY HURT, PAIN, ABUSE OR LET DOWN THAT I HAVE BEEN HOLDING ON TO IN MY HEART, IN MY SPIRIT, IN MY FLESH AND IN MY INNERMOST BEING.

I RELEASE TODAY AND LET IT GO SO THAT I MAY WALK IN THE NEWNESS OF FREEDOM AND EXPERIENCE ALL THE BLESSINGS AVAILABLE TO ME.

FREEDOM IS MINE TODAY AND I RECEIVE IT IN JESUS NAME...

ଓ FREEDOM TO FORGIVE ଓ

Reflect on your day...

✓ **Did you recite today's Commitment Statement?**
✓ **Did you recite today's Affirmation?**
✓ **Did you take the Day 10 Challenge?**
✓ **Did you share the challenge with someone else?**

Day 11

ୡୡ

Commitment Statement:

Today I embark upon my 11th day's journey of eliminating stinking thinking…10 days from now my thoughts will be less toxic and more abundantly positive! I am fully committed to changing my way of thinking!

TAMING MY TONGUE DAY

Communication is essential in any relationship, with kids, spouses, co-workers, friends, etc. WORDS are POWERFUL; words can either TEAR DOWN or BUILD UP! As a child I remember chanting "sticks and stones may break my bones but names will never hurt me".

It does matter WHAT you say and HOW you say it. Work on communicating effectively and positively, so you can say what you mean without being negative.

On the contrary words can and do hurt. Once spoken it's hard to take them back.

As adults I'm sure by now we realize that it's not necessarily what you say that hurts a person as it is so much in the way it is spoken.

With that said let's work on taming the tongue. Biblical scripture says "...out of the abundance of the heart the mouth speaks" meaning what's in you is what normally comes out of you.

There are so many tongues: boasting tongue, argumentative tongue, manipulating tongue, rude tongue, know-it-all tongue, doubting tongue, complaining tongue, silent tongue, cursing tongue, cynical tongue, judgmental tongue, gossiping tongue, hurtful tongue, bitter tongue, sour tongue and on and on.

How does TAMING OUR TONGUE relate to positive thinking? Simply, listening more as opposed to responding in haste can help tremendously. A cute but true thought...we have two ears for listening and just one mouth for speaking....

☙TAMING MY TONGUE ☙ CHALLENGE

Communication isn't communication until the person that you're talking to understands what it is you are trying to convey.

Listen completely before responding and repeat back to the person what you think you heard them say. This may help in eliminating stinking thinking and curb the tongue that responds in haste from mis-hearing or mis-interpretation.

☙ TAMING MY TONGUE ☙ AFFIRMATION

Today I am thinking before speaking as I realize that my words are powerful and life and death are in the tongue.

Communication isn't communication until the person I'm speaking to understands what it is I'm truly trying to convey.

☙ TAMING MY TONGUE ☙

Reflect on your day...

✓ Did you recite today's Commitment Statement?
✓ Did you recite today's Affirmation?
✓ Did you take the Day 11 Challenge?
✓ Did you share the challenge with someone else?

Day12

ණ෴

Commitment Statement:

Today I embark upon my 12th day's journey of eliminating stinking thinking...9 days from now my thoughts will be less toxic and more abundantly positive! I am fully committed to changing my way of thinking!

FRIENDSHIP DAY

A man that hath friends must show himself friendly: and there is a friend that sticketh closer than a brother.
(Proverbs 18:24 KJV)

Friends are in our lives for a reason, a season or a lifetime.

Did you stop to think that maybe there is more that you could do before relinquishing a long time friend?

This of course takes into consideration that sometimes a relationship needs to be severed, but not in all cases.

Look around and decide which friends deserve to go with you to that next level in your life and which ones do not.

Surround yourself with those who celebrate you and not those who simply tolerate you.

The dictionary defines a friend as someone who is attached to another by feelings of affection or personal regard, gives assistance, supports and is not hostile.

You on the other hand must be all of these things as well.

☙ FRIENDSHIP ☙ CHALLENGE

Put YOURSELF
in someone else's place instead of
putting them in their place.

☙ FRIENDSHIP ☙ AFFIRMATION

I will put myself in another's place
instead of putting them in their place.

If you'll notice, the topics that we have covered do not necessarily pertain to the people we come into contact with but more so what we can do to change the way we think about those interactions.

We're positively eliminating stinking thinking!

☙ FRIENDSHIP ☙

Reflect on your day…

____

____

____

____

____

____

____

____

____

____

✓ **Did you recite today's Commitment Statement?**
✓ **Did you recite today's Affirmation?**
✓ **Did you take the Day 12 Challenge?**
✓ **Did you share the challenge with someone else?**

Day13

ꕥ

Commitment Statement:

Today I embark upon my 13th day's journey of eliminating stinking thinking... 8 days from now my thoughts will be less toxic and more abundantly positive! I am fully committed to changing my way of thinking!

AGAPE DAY

Selfless love of one person for another without sexual implications (especially love that is spiritual in nature) representing human kindness and compassion is defined as Agape.

The greatest command we have been given, is that we love each other as Christ loved the church.

If you desire a little more love show some love today and receive it when it comes back your way.

Other types of love are: unconditional love, romantic love, compassionate love, tough love, erotic love, philos love, sexual love, platonic love, religious love...

ଓ AGAPE CHALLENGE ଓ

GIVE SOME AGAPE LOVE TODAY!!!!
TELL SOMEONE YOU LOVE THEM
(and mean it).

☙ AGAPE AFFIRMATION 1 ☙

**My love is great! I love greatly!
My love is a change agent for hate!
I love above and beyond myself
and it reflects in the love I am shown!
No one can take the love I have
for it is freely given! I am full of love and
overflowing....I am Love!!!!**

☙ AGAPE AFFIRMATION 2☙

**Putting into motion loving those I love,
loving those I like and loving those
who dislike me!**

☙ AGAPE ☙

Reflect on your day...

____

____

____

____

____

____

____

____

____

- ✓ **Did you recite today's Commitment Statement?**
- ✓ **Did you recite today's Affirmation?**
- ✓ **Did you take the Day 13 Challenge?**
- ✓ **Did you share the challenge with someone else?**

Day 14

Commitment Statement:

Today I embark upon my 14th day's journey of eliminating stinking thinking…7 days from now my thoughts will be less toxic and more abundantly positive! I am fully committed to changing my way of thinking!

OPPORTUNITY TO MAXIMIZE DAY

An opportunity is defined as:
A favorable or advantageous circumstance or combination of circumstances.

Maximize simply means to increase or make as great as possible. Nothing hurts more or can compare to the presentation of a once in a lifetime opportunity that slips right through your fingers.

How can I maximize each moment?
By letting go of fear!

Fear paralyzes and causes one to miss out on what is right before them. Fear is simply false evidence appearing real...

Step out on faith when you are presented with opportunity and maximize it in every way possible. Stretch yourself
if you must to meet the need
with boldness and confidence in yourself.

The only one preventing you from moving once you meet opportunity is YOU!

Remember words and thoughts are powerful...call your opportunities in to you daily and then maximize them!

☙ OPPORTUNITY TO MAXIMIZE ☙ CHALLENGE

Take the opportunity to maximize something you are endeavoring to do today.

At work ~ Do something in a greater spirit of excellence!

At home ~ Make a greater dinner, do a greater cleaning...

In the car ~ Take the high road and let someone in purposely or do not acknowledge road rage!

At school ~ Present your project to the very best of your ability in every area!

At church ~ Speak to everyone even those that do not speak to you (with a smile)!

Just own every opportunity to maximize!

☙ OPPORTUNITY TO MAXIMIZE ☙
AFFIRMATION 1

Today is my day of opportunity...Doors are opening up for me and my gifts have already made room...my gifts are leading me through GREAT doors that will take me before GREAT PEOPLE...And when my chance meets my opportunity I won't have to get ready because I AM READY! ~

☙ OPPORTUNITY TO MAXIMIZE ☙
AFFIRMATION 2

If you want an amazing life, you have to surround yourself with amazing people that are doing amazing things; they will encourage you to challenge yourself, to step outside the box and make things happen.

~ Christine Campbell ~

☙ OPPORTUNITY TO MAXIMIZE ☙ PRAYER

TODAY I PRAY FOR FORGIVENESS
FOR ANYTHING THAT I MAY HAVE DONE
THAT COULD BE HINDERING ME FROM MOVING
FORWARD IN MAXIMIZING MY OPPORTUNITIES.

ANY ALT, ANYTHING I'VE SPOKEN IN ANGER, HURT
OR PAIN LORD FORGIVE ME ON THIS DAY.

NOW LORD I DECREE AND DECLARE
THAT EVERY GREAT AND WONDERFUL
OPPORTUNITY THAT YOU HAVE FOR MY LIFE IS
COMING TO ME NOW IN THE NAME OF JESUS!

I COMMAND OPPORTUNITIES TO COME
FROM THE NORTH,
FROM THE SOUTH,
FROM THE EAST
AND FROM THE WEST.

I COMMAND DOORS OF OPPORTUNITY
TO MANIFEST BEFORE ME AND CAUSE ME TO
MAXIMIZE EVERY GIFT AND POTENTIAL THAT YOU
HAVE PLANTED DEEP DOWN WITHIN ME

I SPEAK AN END TO EVERY HINDRANCE
AND AN OPEN DOOR TO EVERY BLESSING!

IN JESUS NAME!

☙ OPPORTUNITY TO MAXIMIZE ☙

Reflect on your day...

____

____

____

____

____

____

____

____

____

____

✓ **Did you recite today's Commitment Statement?**
✓ **Did you recite today's Affirmation?**
✓ **Did you take the Day 14 Challenge?**
✓ **Did you share the challenge with someone else?**

WEEK THREE

Day15

ᘒᘒ

Commitment Statement:

Today I embark upon my 15th day's journey of eliminating stinking thinking...6 days from now my thoughts will be less toxic and more abundantly positive! I am fully committed to changing my way of thinking!

ARMOUR UP!

How are you protecting your mind from negative thoughts? Try putting on the full armour!

Armour is defined as any defensive covering worn to prevent injury to the body in battle. Most battles incorporate the mental and the physical/stamina!

REMEMBER the key is to keep control of your thoughts.

Put on the (helmet of salvation). A helmet protects or covers your thinking from stepping out of the will for your life.

Guard your mind from attacks that try to filter through and do not allow yourself to be a garbage can for others negative thoughts or information, you are not a dumping portal. Protect YOURSELF!

Remember to (*shod your feet*). Shod means to protect or cover your walk. You can equip yourself by going places that you are celebrated and not only tolerated. Protect YOURSELF!

A *breastplate* is twofold. It is a covering for your chest/heart as well as a cover for your back. Why continue to go places or do things that you know will be a struggle for you in your emotions. Protect your heart. Protect your back. Protect YOURSELF!

Gird yourself. Gird means to surround. Surround yourself with positive influences.

Use your sword. The sword is the word. Remember we talked about life and death being in the tongue? Only say things that will be beneficial to you or someone else.

Only receive things that will be beneficial to you and make daily declarations over your life.
PROTECT YOURSELF!

Last but not least walk in the armour that fits your custom made life.

You cannot walk in the armour that works for someone else, as their battle may not be yours and most likely their armour will not fit.

Find what works for you: songs, scripture, positive people, positive places, sticky note reminders, poems, books, prayer.

Certainly you can operate in your own armour successfully when you are aware of how it can and will work for you.
Hmmm let me see...how many ways can I say this?
PROTECT YOURSELF!

☙ ARMOUR UP! CHALLENGE ☙

Figure out what your armour is! Are you prepared for daily battle? What do you use to protect your mind?

Use your sword (your word). What is your helmet and how are you staying in the will? How do you shod your feet, what places have you stopped going or what people have you stopped being around?

What is your breastplate, how are you protecting your heart and your back? Lastly who are you girded with or surrounded by? Have you armed up today?

☙ ARMOUR UP! AFFIRMATION ☙

Always guard what God gives...as soon as he feeds your spirit be on point so to protect the in-pouring so it doesn't turn into an unwanted outpouring.

I am guarded on every side and every angle I cherish all He's given...I'm protected with His armour!

☙ ARMOUR UP! ☙

Reflect on your day...

____

____

____

____

____

____

____

____

____

____

- ✓ **Did you recite today's Commitment Statement?**
- ✓ **Did you recite today's Affirmation?**
- ✓ **Did you take the Day 15 Challenge?**
- ✓ **Did you share the challenge with someone else?**

Day 16

ஒஒ

Commitment Statement:

Today I embark upon my 16th day's journey of eliminating stinking thinking…5 days from now my thoughts will be less toxic and more abundantly positive! I am fully committed to changing my way of thinking!

GIVE THANKS DAY

Remembering the things that I continue to be thankful for: healing, strength, deliverance, temperance, understanding, family, opportunities, friends, the renewing of my mind, patience, love, support, life, breath, the activities of my limbs, all of the senses, and on and on.

Take some time to focus on the things you do have as opposed to the things that you do not.

Be thankful for new mercies and the opportunity to live another day.

Being thankful means that you have taken the time to reflect and voice what you are thankful for even though things may not be going the way you expected.

Perhaps there's someone in particular who may need to hear "thank you" from you today:

a striving child, a supportive spouse,
a loving friend, an encouraging boss,
a praying intercessor perhaps or
a leader who is interested in
your well being.

☙ GIVE THANKS ☙ CHALLENGE

Take some time out today simply to give thanks. For what you ask? EVERYTHING!!!

Thank someone again...
Thank someone you may have forgotten to thank...

And most importantly thank the Creator for all that he has done and yet continues to do...

☙ GIVE THANKS ☙ AFFIRMATION

I'm thankful today for all that He has done. No one else could have done it better so I'm thankful for the One who has. Thank you Lord for everything great and small.

Have a thoughtfully thankful day....
Be thankful and grateful
for ALL that HE has done! Let's go!

☙ GIVE THANKS ☙

Reflect on your day...

✓ Did you recite today's Commitment Statement?
✓ Did you recite today's Affirmation?
✓ Did you take the Day 16 Challenge?
✓ Did you share the challenge with someone else?

Day 17

ꕥꕥ

Commitment Statement:

Today I embark upon my 17th day's journey of eliminating stinking thinking. 4 days from now my thoughts will be less toxic and more abundantly positive! I am fully committed to changing my way of thinking!

WALK IT OUT DAY!

Let's have some fun today!

Why worry if you're going to pray
and why pray if you're going to worry?
Just walk it out!

Fill your mind in the morning with positive thoughts so that others cannot fill your mind with negative thoughts throughout the day. An idle mind is the enemies' playground...learn to just walk it out!

Fill your mind in the morning with a song or a scripture.

What you feed your mind with is what you will begin to see. When waves of negativity try to filter through just deflect it away by singing your song or fixating on your scripture.

When the "pressures" of life seem to weigh you down they are doing what they have been designed to do "press you".

So don't get pressed or depressed think yourself happy, speak yourself happy and walk it out!

☙ WALK IT OUT ☙ CHALLENGE

Get a song in your spirit to help you along your day...let this be your walk it out song.

Think of some personal scriptures that will make you happy and think on them (tell yourself things that you know will make you happy).

☙ WALK IT OUT ☙ AFFIRMATION

When worry comes my way...
I'll sing a song and walk it out.

When sorrow seems to gray...
I'll just pray and walk it out.

The pressures of life come to press me
But I won't get pressed or depressed

I will think myself happy, speak myself
happy And walk it on out.

☙ WALK IT OUT ☙

Reflect on your day...

____

____

____

____

____

____

____

____

____

____

- ✓ **Did you recite today's Commitment Statement?**
- ✓ **Did you recite today's Affirmation?**
- ✓ **Did you take the Day 17 Challenge?**
- ✓ **Did you share the challenge with someone else?**

Day18

ஒ

Commitment Statement:

Today I embark upon my 18th day's journey of eliminating stinking thinking. 3 days from now my thoughts will be less toxic and more abundantly positive! I am fully committed to changing my way of thinking!

ଓ ENCOURAGE A CHILD DAY ଓ

Over time we have learned to encourage ourselves but who is encouraging the children? Have you ever stopped to wonder just who is training up the children these days? Parents, grandparents, extended family, teachers, church, community and society.

With so much going on in the world it really makes you wonder if we've done our part or if children have decided to rear themselves?

Well let's look at it from another perspective...
It really does take a village to raise a child.
Education is not what it used to be, prayer was taken out of the schools, activities are being stripped away, learning is becoming a chore and certainly times have changed.

And while we may not be able to "all go back to the ole' time way" we can go back to each one teach one.

Training simply means to coach or prepare into a mode of behavior or performance especially by repetition.

In most every culture children are taught to honor their parents, however if they do not have parents or have somehow grown up without being taught this, then they have been done a disservice. Let's teach the children by leading them, encouraging them, offering love, support, and a listening ear (on a regular basis).

☙ ENCOURAGE A CHILD ☙ CHALLENGE

Do something encouraging for a child today. Whose child? Your child or another's. Make an impact in some kind of way.

Show some love, share life, share your story, ask them what their vision is, who they admire, what they would like to do.

Let's pay some attention now so it hopefully will not cost later. We're positively eliminating stinking thinking.

☙ ENCOURAGE A CHILD ☙ AFFIRMATION

I'm making a difference!
I'm training up a child in the way that he/she should go. I'm showing them how to honor their parents and sowing a seed of love. I'm paying attention now so that hopefully it will not cost later.

☙ ENCOURAGE A CHILD ☙

Reflect on your day...

____

____

____

____

____

____

____

____

____

____

- ✓ **Did you recite today's Commitment Statement?**
- ✓ **Did you recite today's Affirmation?**
- ✓ **Did you take the Day 18 Challenge?**
- ✓ **Did you share the challenge with someone else?**

Day 19

ஒஒ

Commitment Statement:

Today I embark upon my 19th day's journey of eliminating stinking thinking... 2 days from now my thoughts will be less toxic and more abundantly positive! I am fully committed to changing my way of thinking!

VISION DAY

And Jehovah answered me, and said,
"Write the vision, and make it plain upon tablets, that he may run that readeth it. For the vision is yet for the appointed time, and it hasteth toward the end, and shall not lie: though it tarry, wait for it; because it will surely come,
it will not delay." Habakkuk 2:2-3 KJV

Vision: The manner in which one sees or perceives something. Writing: The actual forming of words on a surface such as paper with a pen or instrument.

An interesting thought:
BE ~ DO ~ HAVE
Once you become what God has called you to BE, You can then DO what He has called you to do and HAVE what God has called you to have.

≈ VISION ≈
Write the Vision

What could you see yourself doing but have not ventured out to do? Perhaps a calling or gift that people keep encouraging you to try your hand at?

What is that dream that you keep pushing to the back burner? What is your vision, goal or idea and have you taken the time to extensively write it down? Have you placed a start or completion date on it yet? Have you spoken it into the atmosphere? Can you see yourself doing it? And lastly are you surrounded by promoters of your vision?

ℭ VISION CHALLENGE ℭ

Write down your dream or vision and be specific. Place a realistic start date, goal, deadline and a completion date for your project.

Open your eyes to what's around you so that when things are presented to you, you will recognize the provisions of your vision being met.

ℭ VISION AFFIRMATION ℭ

Once you become what God has called you to be. You can then do what He has called you to do, and have what God has called you to have. Write the vision!

NO MATTER WHAT YOU DO *"someone"* is going to talk about you.

"Do not allow the 'criticism' of NAYSAYERS cause you to abort your vision". TD Jakes

☙ VISION ☙

Reflect on your day…

✓ Did you recite today's Commitment Statement?
✓ Did you recite today's Affirmation?
✓ Did you take the Day 19 Challenge?
✓ Did you share the challenge with someone else?

Day 20

ঞ্জ

Commitment Statement:

Today I embark upon my 20th day's journey of eliminating stinking thinking...1 day from now my thoughts will be less toxic and more abundantly positive! I am fully committed to changing my way of thinking!

PERSECUTION PERMITS PROMISE

Strategically this day was placed just before our day of victory as persecution usually comes just before the promise or the victory!

Persecution is the systematic mistreatment of an individual or group by another group. The infliction of suffering, harassment, isolation, fear, pain or exclusion.

With any elevation comes resistance and most times in the form of persecution.

In leadership someone may not like the way you walk, the way you smile, the way you operate in excellence, the way you keep it moving (K.I.M.) without giving up, the way you can discern a situation, the love you have for people, the way you keep the peace...and on and on.

What we sometimes fail to realize is that this comes along with the position. Different levels bring different devils.

If no one has ever told you, I'm telling you today what to expect. There's no getting around it, no avoiding it, no stopping it...*it is what it is*.

If everyone is always in agreement with what you do then perhaps you are surrounded by people pleasers.

What is a people pleaser?
Someone who does something just to satisfy the desires of others. With every opportunity to advance, there is also a price that comes along with it.

☙ PERSECUTION PERMITS ☙ PROMISE CHALLENGE

Today release your stinking thinking as it relates to someone who opposes you or your position in leadership.

Know that they were designed with you in mind and that the fight is within and not without.

BEFORE being persecuted today tell yourself:

"I am fully armored and dangerous and realize that I wrestle not against flesh and blood, but against spiritual wickedness in high places!"

☙ PERSECUTION PERMITS ☙ PROMISE AFFIRMATION

Persecution is only effective to the degree that you need acceptance from those who talk about you....if you don't need acceptance ignore them. Bishop I V Hilliard

☙ PERSECUTION PERMITS ☙ PROMISE

Reflect on your day...

✓ **Did you recite today's Commitment Statement?**
✓ **Did you recite today's Affirmation?**
✓ **Did you take the Day 20 Challenge?**
✓ **Did you share the challenge with someone else?**

Day 21

Commitment Statement:

Today I embark upon my 21st day journey of eliminating stinking thinking. From now on I will put forth the effort to ensure my thoughts are less toxic and more abundantly positive! I am fully committed to changing my way of thinking and will repeat this challenge for as long as it takes!

VICTORY DAY

In the words of Kirk Franklin...
"Put ya hands up, up, ya got ya hands up? We just broke down the statistic of 80-90% of negative thinking and turned it into a daily process of POSITIVE THINKING by eliminating stinking thinking!

And while today should certainly be a day of celebration keep in mind that without continued work in the area of positivity it is so easy to slip right back into an old state of mind. No matter the age this particular way of thinking, operating or renewing daily must become a lifestyle change.

What is victory?
Victory is success in overcoming a difficult situation or an obstacle. Victory is also a success in a contest against an enemy or opponent, or success in a particular contest or battle that is won.

☙ VICTORY AFFIRMATION ☙

I am positively convinced
there's a winner in me!

☙ VICTORY CHALLENGE ☙

Your only challenge today
is to walk in total and
complete *victory*!

ଓ VICTORY ଓ

Reflect on your day...

- ✓ Did you recite today's Commitment Statement?
- ✓ Did you recite today's Affirmation?
- ✓ Did you take the Day 21 Challenge?
- ✓ Did you share the challenge with someone else?
- ✓ Did you complete the challenge?

CHALLENGER TESTIMONIES

AND

ACKNOWLEDGEMENTS

CHALLENGER TESTIMONIES AND ACKNOWLEDGEMENTS
FROM FACEBOOK GROUPS CHALLENGES 1, 2, AND 3

CHALLENGER TESTIMONIES AND ACKNOWLEDGEMENTS FROM FACEBOOK GROUPS CHALLENGES 1, 2, AND 3

CHALLENGE 1 & 3

Paul E Tenant
I have been stuck in negative thinking for quite some time and I just felt like there was no way out but who came to my rescue, my FB friends from way back and I appreciated every minute of it Good looking out LOC, Victory is God's then ours!!!!

CHALLENGE 2 & 4

Rhonda White-Young
This 21 Day Journey for me can be summed up in two quotes... King said "Take the first step in faith. You don't have to see the whole staircase, just take the first step". I loved every bit of the steps to eliminating Stinking Thinking. My post it notes are my constant reminder that really Day 22 is just the beginning. This was a GREAT challenge because it gave me something to be accountable to daily and helped me to see life even more differently through a different set of lenses. It was GREAT to be a part of a team bringing me to my second quote that sums it up that "Individual glory is insignificant when compared to achieving VICTORY as a team".
Whoo-Whoo~~~~~~ CELEBRATE VICTORY EVERYDAY!!!

CHALLENGE 3

Sharon Pinkard Wilson Day 13 was a kicker for me. I had to let go of some people I thought were my friends and it was really hard because I felt guilty and sad because I had to let them go I realized they were not good for me anymore the season had passed.

CHALLENGE 3

Sandia Harges Day 17 Freedom to forgive was my favorite, because there were some people I needed to forgive in order to move forward. The challenge (all of them) seemed to come exactly when I needed them. Thanks Rachon, I look forward to participating in other challenges.

CHALLENGER TESTIMONIES AND ACKNOWLEDGEMENTS FROM FACEBOOK GROUPS CHALLENGES 1, 2, AND 3

CHALLENGE 3

Lavon Williams-Green

Blessings Rachon CubanDiva Thomas
I would have to say my favorite challenge was ~Victory
I say that not because it is the end, but the beginning to a more positive me. Again, I say thank you for having the mindset for such an enriching course on Face book. I loved how well constructed the course set-up, the interaction with the other members, showing we all have the love of God in our hearts. I am going to stay more positive and prayerful, praying for you, please pray for me.

CHALLENGE 2

Michaele Brown

Hi my fellow challengers! This was indeed a wonderful journey. My prayer for each of you is that you would apply what you've learned from this challenge to other areas in your life. It's not enough just to have knowledge of something. We have to have an Implementation Plan. So set your goal, write down your daily strategy, and execute! Let's Go!

CHALLENGE 2 & 3

Robin LadyBird Strong-Robinson

Greetings 2 all my fellow Challengers, I got in on the tail end so I was not able 2 absorb the full 21 days. Yet I have 2 say for the short time I did participate it has truly helped me 2 b more aware of my thoughts & how I tend 2 process & act on them. I thank all of u 4 allowing me the opportunity 2 b a part of something not only positive but also powerful! Rachon, if & when u begin the next 21 days please keep me posted I want 2 reap the whole process... blessing 2 all of u, LadyBird.

Thank you for taking

the

21 Day Positivity Challenge!

Please send all questions, correspondence and testimonies to: The 21 Day Positivity Challenge to Eliminate Stinking Thinking email address: ***the21daypctest@hotmail.com***

www.ingramcontent.com/pod-product-compliance
Ingram Content Group UK Ltd.
Pitfield, Milton Keynes, MK11 3LW, UK
UKHW041933190726
13854UKWH00004B/1573

9 781105 968440